Release Your Anchor

An Inspiring Short Story of Triumph over Personal, Professional, and Spiritual Hurricanes

Dr. Paulette Howard Burney, PhD

(Release Your Anchor)
Copyright © 2012 by (Dr. Paulette Howard Burney, PhD)

All rights reserved. No part of this book may be reproduced or transmitted in any form or by any means without written permission from the author.

ISBN: 13: 978-0615743455

Dedication

This book is dedicated to all those who will allow love, peace, hope, faith, and tranquility to guide their hearts, mind, and soul. Release your anchor which should be rooted and grounded in the Word of God because his promises are truth and his Word is not void.

Dr. Paulette Howard Burney

Success is to be measured not so much by the position that one has reached in life as by the obstacles which he has overcome.

Booker T. Washington

Table of Contents

Contents 5-6
Preface 7
Introduction 8-9
The Hen(Woman):The Story 10-13
The Rooster (Man) 14-17
The Snake (Deceiver) 18-19
The Snake's Influences on Hen 20-21
Optimist and Pessimist (Cockerels-Male Sons) .. 22-25
Career Planning: Personal, Professional, and Spiritual 26-27
Hen's Hurricanes 28-35
The Divorce 36-39
Hen's New Beginning 40-43
Optimists Independence 44-45
Pessimist (Victory) Struggles 46-48
Hen's Hurricane 49-52
After the Divorce: Celibacy 53-54
A New Rooster of Oneness 55
Discussion 55-56
Conquering Your Fears 57-58
Change for the Better 59-60
Humility 61-62
Pride 63-64

Pessimistic Behavior	65-69
Renewing My Mind Checklist	67-68
Optimistic Behavior	69-70
Handwriting on the Heart	71-75
Forgiveness	76-77
Love	78-79
Faith	80-81
Peace	82
Hope	84-84
Tranquility	85-86
Discussion	87-89
Five Steps to Releasing Your Anchor: Personal and Professional Development	90
Spiritual Development	91-93
Defining Your Success	94-96
Dialog	97-98
Development Theory	99-100
Theory Application	101-103
Womb Theory	101-107
Exercises	108-116
Certification	117
The Promise	118-120
Conclusion and References	121-122
About the Author and Words of Truth	123-131

Preface

One autumn chilly day, while sitting on the floor in front of a warm cozy fire, "Humility" was inspired by God to write this short story. It is written to uplift those who may be facing obstacles in life, or those who will face obstacles in life and need to make positive decisions to overcome the hurricanes in his or her life.

When reading this short story, open your heart and mind. Allow the words to place an "anchor" in your soul to combat all hurricanes in your life forever.

Always look forward in your life. Never let your past haunt you. You are not a victim of any circumstance. You are a voice of love, faith, hope, peace, and tranquility.

Introduction

Release Your Anchor is an inspiring short story written as a parable to uplift those who may be going through obstacles in life. It is a motivational story of five characters, the hen, rooster, two cockerels, and the snake.

The hen is named Humility a metaphor for a woman. The rooster is Pride who is a man, two cockerels; Optimist and Pessimist later called *Victory* are the sons of rooster and hen. *"Hurricanes"* is a metaphor for obstacles faced whether on the job, relationship, financial, health, or spiritual peace of mind.

The *"Anchor"* is your spiritual man, where you go for strength for what you want on the job, relationships, the family or community you live in.

In the story, the characters are faced with unexpected hurricanes. When you come to the hand writing in your heart, you will understand for yourself how to deal with hurricanes. When you are able to deal with hurricanes, your life will become less stressful; you will experience more success (as you define it) in your personal and professional life.

This story is written for all ages, and it takes less than one hour to read, however in getting an understanding of the meaning of these words they can change your life forever.

The Hen (Woman): The Story

ONCE, in a land far away, there lived five characters, a hen (Woman/Humility), referred to as a wife, a rooster (Man/Pride), the husband, two cockerels Optimist and Pessimist/ Victory (Sons of the hen and rooster), and the snake (the deceiver).

In elementary school the hen had low self-esteem. She was in E-F group in school. Groups were ranked from A being highest and F, the lowest. As a child, the Hen was called strange and frowned upon because she was grey headed. She was the middle child reared in a single family home with three other siblings, two girls, and one brother. The Hen's mother and father separated when she was a newborn returning from the hospital with only her mother. The dream, the Hen had changed her perspective about life. She understood that she did not have to worry about what other people thought about her because she was a child of God, saved by his grace.

She had an *anchor* in her life to surpass all hurricanes. You will later read about the hurricanes of her life and how she overcame them.

In the Hen's dream, she saw what John described in the book of (Revelation 1: 13-15). She saw the Son of Man wearing a white long robe, his hair was as wool and white as snow, his skin was the color of burned brass, and his eyes as the flame of fire. He held the Hen's hand and walked her through purple curtains (symbolic of grace). He walked her to the roof top of her mother's home and sat there with her. They looked up into the stars, and he disappeared.

One day, two elementary school teachers came together with the hen and explained how her academic performance allowed her to be placed in C group instead of E-F. Later, in the school year, the hen was asked to perform as the star character in the play, the *Little Red Hen*. This academic school year made a positive impact in the hen's life. Once the hen reached Middle School, she had advanced to A-B group. The Hen was a great singer. She led her community choir for many years. She was a member of Girl Scouts of America, and 4-H club. In high school, she was a member of the National Honor Society and Recognized as Who's Who Among American Students, a member of the Student Council, and Officer of the High School Chorus. She was accepted into college, however married the Rooster and delayed starting college.

The Hen wanted to become married because from a child she believed in (Luke 12: 31), which she should seek first the kingdom of God and his righteous and all other things would be added unto her. She believed that marriage was honorable and the bed undefiled (Hebrews 13:4). The Hen was a very humble wife, who married in her youth, who enjoyed being married and caring for her rooster and cockerels. The Hen's plans to attend college were delayed whenever her husband, the rooster joined the U.S. military.

The Rooster

The Rooster, the oldest male child, was reared in a single family home with three other siblings, one girl, and two boys. The Rooster was very intelligent. The Rooster and the hen's mother were close friends. He was attending college, however left college to marry the hen. The Rooster was older than the Hen. He had experienced sexual relations with many females, one being much older and experienced, with child. The Rooster was very jealous. However, he appeared to love the hen very much. The Hen and Rooster attended church regularly together. They communicated often and shared the Bible.

After a few years of marriage, the rooster joined the military. The Rooster left for Basic Training in the military. The hen bore the rooster's first cockerel (Optimist). The rooster took great pride in serving his country and providing shelter for his wife and son.

However, the Rooster's attitude changed. The "Snake" persuaded the rooster, that he was too young to be married. The Snake deceived the rooster to believe that all other women were more beautiful, intelligent, overall better than his wife, the hen. The Rooster moved the Hen and Optimist to Europe with him. However, he listened to the snake and turned away from his family. The Rooster started drinking, staying out all night, and having extra-marital affairs.

One day, the prayers of the Hen and intercessors were heard. The Rooster repented of his sins and started to respect his family again. Yet, the snake was not finished with the rooster. He told the Rooster that he would find his house unclean and he would enter again. The Rooster brought his family to another location in Europe to live. Yet, his mistress was there awaiting him.

> *You are given the freedom to make the right choices for your life. Make the positive choice.*

The Rooster's behavior never changed. Hen bore him their second cockerel, (Pessimist). Rooster returned home to his family after Pessimist was born. The snake's influence on Rooster was so strong that he became violent toward Hen.

Be sober, be vigilant; because your adversary the devil, as a roaring lion, walketh about, seeking whom he may devour (1Peter 4:8).

The Snake

The snake is the deceiver and the accuser of the brethren (Revelation 12:10). He is the one who controls the natural and carnal man because as humans we give him this authority. The only way to keep the snake under submission is "the Blood of Jesus." Never give the snake dominion over your life, however call him out by his name and plead the "Blood of Jesus" over your hurricane.

The snake brings hurricanes in your life. However, your spiritual man has the power to control all hurricanes. When you see a hurricane coming, prepare yourself for the attack. Do not just let it happen without putting up a spiritual fight. You can win. Keep the faith. No matter what the situation looks like in the carnal, claim the victory in the spiritual realm.

Focus on your positive outcome and not the hurricanes. For every hurricane, create a positive outcome using the Word of God. Find the scripture which reflects what you are going through and read it daily.

You may need to fast and pray to conquer the snake, but do not become dismayed because greater is he that is in you than he that is in the carnal hemisphere.

Do not believe everything you hear or see. The snake will come to deceive many in the end time.

Keep your anchor in the ready position because you must be prepared for all forms of hurricanes. Do not become conformed to this world, but become transformed by the renewing of your mind, heart, and soul.

> *And they overcame him by the blood of the Lamb, and by the word of their testimony... (Revelation 12:3).*

The Snake's Influence on the Hen

The Hen started the University in Europe during Rooster's first military tour. She met wonderful friends and prayer partners. The Hen became wellness oriented. She started a jogging and Bible study group. She became a career woman. She loved and cared for Optimist and Rooster.

Her day began at 6 a.m. and ended 11 p.m. daily, to pray, exercise, prepare meals, care for the cockerels, and work outside of the home. Family dinner was mandatory and Bible study held weekly. The Hen was able to manage her time well between family, friends, and work.

The acknowledgement of Rooster's first affair started with a phone call at Hen and Rooster's home. Hen wanted a divorce because rooster confessed to the adultery. Hen was afraid it would happen again. However, in humility, the Hen humbled herself to the

Word of God (Matthew 5:32). She understood that it was not intended for a man and woman to divorce.

Yet, the snake played on the Hen's emotions often. The snake made the Hen believe that she was ugly, not intelligent, unworthy of happiness, and life. Whenever Hen learned that she was pregnant with their second child she was so depressed. Rooster was with so many women and she felt so alone. She drove herself off one night to a hotel to commit suicide; however she could not do it.

Whenever Hen told rooster about her depression, he laughed and said, I thought you were out with another man. Rooster left his family and did not return until their second son was born. Hen, welcomed him back with loving arms. However, rooster became violent toward Hen whenever she confronted him about his other women, drinking, and staying out all night.

Optimist and Pessimist (*Victory*)

Optimist from a newborn was a quiet cockerel. He was playful and never cried much. He was a cockerel who always enjoyed learning about other cultures. Perhaps, he enjoyed learning about other cultures because he experienced many European cultures as a child. Optimist always listened to Hen and Rooster. He loved Pessimist very much and helped Hen with caring for him.

Optimist enjoyed playing baseball and he was a member of Boy Scouts of America. Rooster did spend some time with Optimist as a child until the tours in Europe ended. He was always a good student in school. Hen was never called to the school for any disciplinary actions against Optimist. He graduated from high school and received the Presidential Award for Community Service. He was very different from Pessimist from newborn to adulthood.

Pessimist (*Victory*)

Pessimist from a newborn would awake everyone shaking his crib. He actually shook the crib so much that he shook the bolts apart one day. When going for walks to feed the ducks, he would scream at the ducks if they ran away from him. He always wanted to be the center of attention. Pessimist was spoiled because he was the baby in the family and the youngest child.

During Pessimist's first grade school year, Hen and Rooster were told that Pessimist was dyslectic. However, based on his standardized test scores he was above average in his core subjects. Further researched revealed he needed reading glasses. Most of Pessimist's childhood was spent in the United States. He did not enjoy learning about different cultures. Pessimist behavior in school was poor. Hen home schooled Pessimist to receive his high school diploma.

Rooster did not spend any time with Pessimist as a child. Rooster was still in touch with his mistress and unsure if he wanted to be married. The separation of the family made an impact on the behavior of Hen and Rooster's sons. Although, both sons were in the home with both parents, Hen was not able to make the changes alone. She needed the support of Rooster for the boys too become strong productive citizens.

If you have a man in your life that disrespects you, ask him this question. Do you love yourself? If the answer is yes, reply," Love me as much as you love yourself." If the answer is no, reply, "Let us build a relationship teaching us to love one another with a love that is unselfish and unconditional." Each individual should focus on him or herself in a positive way and respect the vision another person has towards completing their individual career goals.

A house divided shall not stand. Children must have the support and love of both parents who are teaching the same values, morals, and principles.

Career Planning: Personal, Professional, and Spiritual

The Hen's career plan was implemented during different stages of her hurricanes. The Hen became a part of the management team of her organization. Her new career plan included the following:

(1) God First

(2) Complete Associate Degree

(3) Stay Happily Married

(4) Complete Bachelors Degree in Business Administration

(5) Management Position with an Organization

(6) Become a School Teacher

(7) Complete Master's Degree in Business Administration

(8) Graduate Kids from High School

(9) Start a Business

(10) Become a College Professor

(11)Send Kids to College

(12)Complete Doctoral Degree

(13)Become a College Administrator

(14)Write and Publish Books and Articles

Hen's career plan was a journey and she faced many hurricanes. When reading about Hen's hurricanes find your anchor and release it.

> *Life is filled with ups and downs. You must decide how to get up whenever you fall down. You can make it if you keep the faith. Never give up on your dreams.*

Hen's Hurricanes

Hen had another dream, before leaving Europe. She dreamed of being in a black pit. Inside of this pit she saw herself having turned away from her first love. That first love was God.

Rooster sent Hen and their two sons to live with his mother in a three bedroom apartment, where she shared the same room with her two sons. Hen was unhappy. Optimist was in school and Hen waited until he completed school before moving away to live with her mother. Rooster was in Korea now with his woman. He had never stopped seeing her or wanting to be with her. Hen could not see how she would ever meet her career goals. Hen was not able to attend college. She could not find employment, she had no income, and she felt hopeless.

While living with her mother, Hen's step father was shot in the front yard of the home. The men who shot him were never captured. Hen was afraid for the life of her cockerels. Whenever she told Rooster about this, he did not care how she felt. Hen continued to pray, but she was becoming more and more depressed. She was now living in a two bedroom home with ten other people. Her brother and his family moved back with her mother while Hen and her cockerels were there. All that Hen could do was take care of her two cockerels. Rooster did not want her to have an apartment. Hen wanted to give up.

The Snake came to Hen and told her, Rooster does not love you or your cockerels. He is only concerned about himself, so what are you going to do? For the first time in Hen's life she allowed the Snake to alter her thinking.

She met a guy and had an affair with him. Hen told Rooster about it and he replied, "I forgive you because I was in Korea with my woman."

Hen's heart was saddened because she did not meet her first career goal and that was God first. However, Hen and Rooster both agreed they would have a fresh start in their marriage once he returned from Korea. However, she remembered, she had an *anchor*.

> *God will forgive our sins and place them into the sea of forgetfulness, never to remember them again (Psalms 103:12)*

Hen, Rooster, Optimist, and Pessimist, are one family again, under the same roof. The Hen did not forget about her career plan she made almost 24 months ago. The Hen was enrolled in college, a mother, and career woman again. Rooster told hen, if she ever got out of line, he had a gun to place her back in line.

One Sunday afternoon, Hen and the boys had returned from church. Rooster heard Hen on the telephone speaking to one of her friends about his youngest brother wanting to come live with them. Hen was not in agreement with Rooster because his brother was struggling with substance abuse. Hen felt it would be better for his brother to get professional help. She did not feel it was good for him to be around their two cockerels. His brother also wanted to bring his girlfriend to live with him. Rooster told Hen, this is my house and I make the decision of who lives here.

Rooster placed a gun to Hen's head because she was talking about the situation to a friend who both of them knew and respected. Hen called the police and Rooster was locked up in jail overnight. Hen did not place any charges against Rooster.

Hen was hysterical. Her mother wanted her to leave with the cockerels. Hen decided she would not let this hurricane prevent her from reaching her fourth career goal.

Hen learned that Rooster was still in contact with his former mistress. She found the telephone bill and called her. Hen was very upset. The snake came to Hen and told her, "Go get you a real man, you do not need to continue to put up with *Pride*, you can make it on your own. "

Hen knew her personal goal of Staying Happily Married was at risk. However, she listened to the Snake, because she did not believe that *Pride* loved her or wanted to have a family any more.

Rooster and Hen were able to live under the same roof with their children. However, Hen was more determined than ever to complete her career plan and be set free. Hen missed the mark again; she did not put

God First. During her state of depression, she meets a man. She does not tell Rooster about him. Rooster does everything he can to find out if and who Hen is seeing. One day, he learns what he thinks is the truth, yet says he wants to remain married.

Hen understands the importance of following her career plan. She knew that if she missed the first goal, she would not be successful at any other goals. Hen went back to the *hand writing on her heart*. The anchor was still in the same place, although the hurricanes continued to rage in her life.

Hen and Rooster separates. Hen is a manager within an organization. Career Goal Six is met. The Snake is within the organization. Hen is Sexual Harassed and Discriminated Against. Hen is retaliated against and terminated from her position. Hen is working toward goals six thru nine simultaneously. Hen started her first business and taught her first college course within thirty days of being wrongfully terminated from her position as manager.

Hen was being called to the high school with good reports about Optimist. However at the Middle School, Pessimist was struggling with improper classroom behavior and a few less than average grades.

Hen's career expands into multiple positions. She settles for a full-time Instructor position with a local college. The family was attending church together; however Hen sensed something was not right with Rooster.

Rooster came to live with Hen whenever she moved in her Management position. However, Rooster was staying away from home and never spending any time with Hen and the cockerels.

Hen asked Rooster to go to counseling; however he refused to do so. Hen, told Rooster that whatever he was doing in the dark was going to come to the light.

And it did. Hen went through one year of humiliation of an affair between Rooster and a recruit which almost cost him his career.

Hen was totally emotional an upset about the situation. Yet, she never spoke against Rooster. He explained they would get through all of this and put this behind them.

At this point Hen, had built a stronger personal relationship with God. She had asked God to reveal to her what was really going on with Rooster. He did not want to go further in the Word of God. Prophecy was given that he would become a pastor, however he said, I am not ready for this. Rooster continued to refer to his past. He told Hen, you do not know the man you are married to. Rooster would not forgive himself of his past. Hen was tired of all of the ups and downs. She wanted peace in her life no matter what the cost.

The Divorce

Rooster told Hen he would move some of the household goods and she would follow him later to move the other household goods to their new military duty station. Rooster told Hen to come by the attorney's office to sign papers to Quit Claim Deed the house over to her. Whenever she arrived at the attorney's office, she was asked to sign her divorce decree and pay over $200.00 in child support.

Hen was devastated that goal three would not be met. She could not be happily married to someone who did not want to be married to her. She felt betrayed, yet relief of not experiencing future heart ache and pain. The pain she felt will never go away because this is what it feels like whenever you lose someone that you care about dearly and want to spend the rest of your life with.

Hen could feel the wind blowing harder than ever. She could not distinguish the night from day. But one thing Hen knew is her soul was *anchored.* She might have to cry sometimes, she may not know where her next meal would come from, or how she would pay her bills, but she knew that her God would not leave her or forsake her.

Optimist stayed with Hen. Pessimist, now 12 years old went to live with Rooster after the divorce. Hen encouraged Optimist to stay in college; however he dropped out and took a job. Yet, Optimist was independent and lived in his own apartment.

Hen started to working toward goal eleven. She was focused and determined to meet this goal, now that she had no distractions. However, Hen was faced with financial hardship. Her full-time Instructor position was reduced to varied hours. Hen did not know where her next meal would come from. Hen had given over twenty years of her life to a man who left her in the wind.

Hen always believed in setbacks as an opportunity for strength, development, and growth based on the story of Job. Job lost everything, yet, he was favored by God and blessed in his later years more than the first (Job 42: 12).

Hen always wanted to become a Teacher as her first career choice. So Hen pursued and became a certified public school teacher. Hen was not facing financial hardship. However, she was alone and a long way away from her family. Pessimist came back to live with Hen. He was disobedient and in trouble at school. Hen felt stress and ashamed of Pessimist's behavior. So she decided to move back to her home state.

> *There is no situation too difficult to resolve, however do not go back to the past if you are working towards a future.*

Hen's New Beginning

Hen is now a single parent in a new state. Hen's career as a teacher was working for her. She relocated to her home state and purchased a new home as a single woman. Hen's experience as an educator within the inner city school was painful.

Hen was determined not to allow Pessimist to destroy everything she had accomplished as a single woman. Pessimist was home schooled and obtained his high school diploma. Goal eight was completed; both boys obtained a high school diploma.

Hen communicated with Pessimistic often and told him how much she loved him. He took the military entrance exam and passed with a high score. He could have chosen any career path of his choice because of his high test score. Hen met all of the requirements for her doctoral degree and graduated. Goal twelve was met.

Hen prayed for resources to improve her business strategy. She wanted to inspire the lives of others by offering housing, leadership, personal and professional development strategies within her community.

Hen's Middle East Career Opportunity allowed her the opportunity to move forward with her business strategy.

Hen returned from the Middle East and moved forward in her career as a College Administrator. Goal thirteen was met. Hen was really off to a great start with her new business strategy and moving forward in her academia career.

Hen was able to reach out to others in her community, sharing to be a blessing to others.

The snake needed to attack Hen because she was doing too much good toward others and touching the lives of others in a positive way. The snake's first attack was on Hen's mind, then her body, her career was taken away, and Pessimist was going in a downward spiral. The snake set a trap for Hen; however the Hen used wisdom to overcome the snares of the snake.

Hen remained professional through her hurricanes. She was asked to leave her job. She provided a great defense for herself, however this was not enough. So, the snake succeeded for a season to prevent the good works provided by Hen. The snake was jealous of Hen. The snake wanted to see Hen fall. The snake wanted Hen to become a victim of circumstance. Hen held on to her dignity and integrity. The snake knew of Hen's passion to reach out to people, to educate, lead, and inspire them to their highest levels of accomplishments.

The same snake that destroyed Hen's marriage is after her children, you and your children. The snake wanted to devour Hen, to stop her purpose.

Hen writes this short story to you because she knows that you can become anchored based on the hand writing in your heart.

> *You must first believe in God and his son, Jesus died and rose on the third day. His bloodshed gives you a second chance. Then believe in yourself; the winds, storms, and hurricanes are fierce but they will not destroy you. (Luke 24:7-12; Matthew 20: 18-19; 1 Corinthians 15:4)*

Optimist's Independence

Optimist was obedient to his parents most of the time. Hen received God's favor and blessings on her life. Hen passed these blessing to her children. Optimist listened to his mother's voice regarding his career. Hen's favor was past to Optimist. This favor allowed him to become financially independent for many years. However, Optimist spent his money on parties, traveling, and women.

Optimist brought back a daughter from his many travels with an empty back account. Yet, his work experience and interpersonal skills with the help of Rooster lands, him a new career path.

Optimist still spends money on fast cars and women. But, he is a good father to his daughter. He believes there is a God; however, living in the city with Rooster and his new wife, Hen rarely get the opportunity to visit. Hen intercedes in prayer for Optimist and her grandchild. Optimist has always been independent, which is a good virtue.

> *Train up a child in the way he should go: and when he is old, he will not depart from it (Proverbs 22:6).*

Pessimist's (Victory's) Struggles

Pessimist returned from the military after completing basic training. He did not go to his first duty station by his choice. The Hen was in the Middle East during this time period. At the age of 17 years old, Pessimist could have retired from the military at the age of 37. Rooster allowed Pessimist to move away from home at the age of 18. Pessimist met a female and several years later, she bore him a daughter. She named the child after Rooster's new wife and her mother. Yet Hen is the main provider for the child. The Hen treated her with so much love and kindness.

Pessimist's issues with his female places him in jail. His disobedience to Hen does not prevent his struggles. However, Hen is totally distorted knowing her child is behind bars.

Hen took care of Pessimist, his girlfriend, and child with no support from Rooster. However, Rooster is working with an attorney to assist Pessimist in being granted a second chance at life. An argument between him and his girlfriend was escalated with the assistance of his girlfriend's family member and two men who came to Pessimist's home. Pessimist in self-defense had a gun and he is being charged with firing the gun as a felony and some other misdemeanor charges. The Hen is now taking care of the baby and the girlfriend. Although, the girlfriend has hurt Hen, she forgave her; continues to love her and the baby very much.

Pessimist never followed the instruction of Hen. He refused to walk the straight and narrow path. His choices were of his free will. Hen continues to pray for Pessimist to walk in the Will of God. She asks, God to bless him and make him a free man.

> *Whoso loveth instruction loveth knowledge: but he that hateth reproof is brutish (Proverbs 12:1).*

Hen's Hurricane

Hen worked so hard all of her life to provide a good home for her cockerels. God gave Hen prophetic words in which she spoke to the policemen once she arrived at Pessimist's home. God was present at the scene and his words were spoken through Hen as if she knew what happened. The Hen spoke the *Prophetic Words of Truth* to the Judge, police officers, and prosecuting attorneys. However they would not release Pessimist from his jail.

The Hen witnessed how a person is proven guilty before innocence. This is the opposite of what our judicial system is about in America. One should be innocent until proven guilty.

The police officers called in a detective to the scene, Hen watched for five hours or more, the detective going around the neighborhood looking for witnesses.

In the 911 call, no one ever stated anyone shooting a gun, only that someone had a gun. Roads were blocked and yellow tape at the scene as if someone had been murdered. No one was killed or harmed.

The detective persuaded witnesses to make statements against Pessimist. He told several witnesses, he wanted this case to stick and put Pessimist away for 25 years.

Pessimist does not understand the type of relationship he is involved in. He does not listen to Hen. Hen had to cast all her cares upon God concerning Pessimist because if not, she would never find peace or tranquility.

The Hen in humility and love allows the girlfriend and the baby to live with her, while her cockerel is in jail. The Hen is providing support to his girlfriend. She wants the best for her and the baby. The girlfriend thought the Hen could change Pessimist. However, Hen could not change him.

Hen explained that change must come from within a person. Even God allowed his son *Jesus* to die for the sins of the world; however every man is given free will. Free will is given to make good choices or bad ones. However, the freedom is through the *Blood of Jesus Christ.* Pessimist sins can be forgiven, and his mind renewed to experience the blessing given to him as an inheritance. Hen cried many nights and interceded in prayer for Pessimist. The intercessor of prayer and fasting was needed because of the heavy strong holds in Pessimist's life. Pessimist is blessed and will be set free.

> *Luke 15: 11-22 Paraphrased: The Prodigal son turned away from God. He went from his Biblical teachings. He is rebellious and must find his way back to God.*

After the Divorce: Hen's Celibacy

Hen decided after the divorce to practice celibacy. She values the holiness and purity of her body. She chose not to date because men thought a date meant she wanted to become sexually involved with them. Hen has spent a decade keeping the practice of celibacy in her heart. However, Hen allowed false prophets in her life whom claimed to be the man sent by God.

She has grown over this period of time understanding men and how many of them chase the *Cookie*. Hen's words of advice are, "If you want a man to respect you, tell him to marry you. Do not have sex with him, tell him you practice celibacy." If he is a real man of God, he will place a ring on your finger before he asks you to have sex with him. If he is not a real Man of God, he will ask to have sex with you and stop coming to see you or taking you out if you do not have sex with him.

Do not believe in the folk tale of making him wait a certain number of dates before having sex with him. Or you need to try it at least once. Once you have sex with him, you may never see him again. It is true there are more women than men. So a man will go to the woman that will give him the sex he wants.

Once he get the sex he wants, he then has no reason to ever want to marry. Allow the man to get to know who you are. He should build a relationship and friendship with you.

Be aware of the gay and bi-sexual movement sweeping our nation. Do not expose yourself to the sexual perversions of this world. Practice abstinence, chastity, holiness, and purity.

A New Rooster of Oneness

Hen has stood at the crossroad numerous times wandering if she would ever find a new Rooster. She decided to ask God to send her a rooster. However no one has appeared. Hen understands the characteristics of a good rooster. She has been told that her standards are too high. Notwithstanding, she has identified the qualities of a good rooster as, follows:

(1)Loves the Lord with All His Heart Mind and Soul

(2)Loves his wife as Christ Loves the Church

Discussion

Is the list of qualities of a good rooster shorter than you imagined?

If a man meets both one and two, he is a man of God and there is no doubt that he will be a good husband. Notwithstanding, actions, speaks louder than words. What has he done to prove his actions?

To answer this question you must turn to your spiritual man. Your husband should be a spiritual man and not a man practicing religion. Do not become deceived by words, but study the Word of God and see if he measures up to God's standard.

Tell yourself, I must never lower my standard, because I am the *Bride of Christ*. I must never look for a husband, my husband will find me. God will not put me back into a relationship filled with hurricanes, after being taken out of the first hurricane.

> *Nevertheless let every one of you in particular so love his wife even as himself; and the wife see that she reverence her husband (Ephesians 5:33).*

Conquering Your Fears

Fear is often the ingredient which prevents one's success. Fear is an attribute from the snake. In the story, each character is depicted as having some fear. For example, if the Hen would have left the Rooster sooner, she could have accomplished her goals sooner. Although she held on to her spiritual values, the marriage ended up in divorce after more than twenty years.

On the other hand, Rooster's fears were from his past. He could not let go of the fears from his past to live a richer life in the future with Hen and their cockerels.

Optimist shows some fear in not completing his college degree. Pessimist could have been afraid of what might happen to him if he served in the military.

The outcomes of each character would be richer, if fear was not a part of the equation. Do not walk in fear, but walk in faith and love.

> *For God has not given us the Spirit of Fear; but of power, and of love and of a sound mind (II Timothy 1:7).*

Change for the Better

Change is needed for improvement. Many view change in a negative way, however without change we would not exist. The change brought about through technological advancement has improved the quality of life for people across the nation. Organizations change their business strategies often for a competitive advantage. No change, no gain.

The divorce was a major change which impacted the lives of each character in the story. Each of the characters survived the change. However, Pessimist was most affected by the change. He could not understand why Hen and Rooster could not remain married as they did when Optimist was a child. The separation of the family broke Pessimist's heart. He no longer had his brother or mother with him. Rooster persuaded him to move away with him because he had all of the money to support him.

Hen explained to Pessimist how much she loved him and wanted their family to be together. However, the change which took place was what Rooster wanted. Hen took Pessimist to counseling session; however he would never open up to the counselor for her to help him.

The move to another state was another change needed for Hen to move on with her life. Getting Pessimist away from his peers and home schooling him was the best change for his life.

> *Change creates a renewing of your mind. A metamorphosis may occur to provide a second chance to someone in need.*

Humility

The Hen is named Humility in the story because her spirit is humble. Hen's pursuit of happiness is what many people hope for today. She wanted to have a career, husband, children, a home, and live happily ever after. Hen's driving force in her life was based on the *anchor* she established as a young girl. She knew humility was an attribute which would take her a very long way in life.

Whenever Hen's hurricanes came before her, many times she remained humble. As long as she stayed humble obtaining and maintaining her first goal was never compromised. Hen often would place others needs before her own. She was portrayed as a *servant leader*. She never had to be the chief in a situation, yet because of her humility she was often asked to become the leader.

In the dream Hen shared as a child, she spoke of the purple curtain symbolic of grace. God gives grace to the humble (I Peter 5:5). Hen reverenced God. She explained how she feared God because she loves him. This type of fear is called wisdom. After each hurricane, Hen was able to accomplish her goals.

> *The fear of the Lord is the instruction of wisdom; and before honor is humility (Proverbs 15:33).*

Pride

Rooster was a man with great pride. A prideful spirit is one that is selfish. Pride always wants to be on top and never serve. Rooster was a vain man in his youth. He had a way of speaking to impress others. His charm always persuaded the women into his arms.

The snake deceived Rooster to believe his vanity was his best attribute. Rooster's desire for woman, lewd, and lascivious behavior persuaded him that Hen was not a woman he wanted to spend the rest of his life with.

Hen wanted Rooster to anchor his soul. She wanted him to renew his spiritual man. She loved Rooster. She wanted him to have a happy and successful future.

> *Pride goeth before destruction,*
> *and a haughty spirit before a fall*
> *(Proverbs 16:18).*

Pessimistic Behavior

Whenever a person is unable to see positive outcomes from their hurricanes, their behavior becomes pessimistic. A pessimist may have a humble or prideful spirit. Pessimistic behavior derives from a negative thought process. Hen had family Bible study in their home. She posted weekly scriptures for her sons to rehearse. Hen constantly reminded Pessimist to obey and honor his parents in the Lord (Ephesians 6:1-2). However, peer pressure was the downfall of Pessimist. He listened to his negative friends instead of Hen.

Hen describes Pessimist as the son who always had negative thoughts. The two of them had many discussions of ways for Pessimist to change his way of thinking. She explained to Pessimist the power of positive thinking and how it could change his life if he applied this simple concept.

Hen wanted Pessimist to look at life from a big picture perspective. She wanted him to open his mind and his heart. Hen gave Pessimist the following to do list to change his heart and mind. She wanted Pessimist to renew his spiritual man and anchor his soul in the Lord. Pessimist is blessed because God's grace is sufficient for him. Hen's love, blessing, and prayers are always with Pessimist.

> *No weapon that is formed against me shall prosper; and every tongue that shall rise against me thee in judgment thou shalt condemn (Isaiah 54:17).*

The renewing of your mind checklist is for everyone who needs to evaluate the position of his or her *anchor*. Application of these six steps will allow you to create a foundation for your soul.

Renewing My Mind Checklist

1. Believe that God the Father sent his Son Jesus to die for our sins and on the third he rose so that we may have eternal life. (John 3:16-17; Romans 5:8; 1John 4:9)
2. Confess your sins. (Romans 10:10; 1Timothy 6:13
3. Repent of my sins daily so that the carnal may dies for my spiritual man to live.
4. Become baptized by being immersed in water symbolic of the old man's death and the birth of your new spiritual man.
5. Pray daily(Matthew 6:9-13) Read daily (Psalms 37: 4-5 ; Matthew: 17:20, Mark 12:30-31; Romans 13:8, Galatians 5:14; Mark 11:23-26, John 13:34; John 15:12-17)
6. Do not socialize with negative people or allow them into your home for the cause of confusion (I Timothy 5:13)

7. Stay employed or in College to ensure you keep your mind focused on positive things (I Timothy 5:8).
8. Whenever a negative thought comes to your mind, state, "I rebuke this evil thought by the Blood of Jesus." Keep silent if you cannot speak these words.
9. Weekly communicate with Spiritual minded people and call upon them when you need to talk to someone.

Optimistic Behavior

The power of positive thinking is a result of one's optimistic behavior. An optimistic person is one who can see the light at the end of the tunnel no matter how threatening the hurricane. Practicing optimistic behavior ensures you will not destroy your life or the lives of others.

Optimist being the older son was more responsible. He was six years older than Pessimist. He listened to Hen and took her advice as a child. Optimist was humble in many ways and inherited some of the attributes of Hen.

Optimist always chose friends who were positive. He was called a bully during his Elementary school years because of his size. However, Optimist was not a bully. He cared about people and was never in any fights at school.

During his teenage years, he was very active in children church. In high school, he was a member of the band. His teachers both male and female often complimented Hen, about the very positive outlook Optimist had on life and his ability to do well in all subjects in high school.

Notwithstanding, Rooster always found fault in Optimist. Optimist cared for Hen whenever hurricanes attached her. He would not leave Hen alone after the divorce. Because of his devotion to his mother and obedience to his parents he is blessed.

> *...Behold, to obey is better than sacrifice ... (I Samuel 15:22).*

Handwriting on the Heart

The handwriting on Hen's heart is where her anchor became placed on her soul. The hurricanes were fierce in Hen's life. Hen never focused on the hurricanes because she lived by faith and not by sight.

Hen was always lead by wisdom to overcome her hurricanes. She always used the ingredients shelved in the Holy Words of God. There are many examples in the story open for discussion to show how Hen's heart and soul are anchored.

Hen felt betrayed by Rooster. She felt that she would never be beautiful or smart enough for him to love her. Hen wanted to commit suicide because she had lost her first love. She had placed her heart and trust in Rooster instead of God. Rooster's repeated affairs, the last act of violence when Rooster placed the gun to her head; changed her outlook on life. Hen thought she was about to die, however at that moment, whenever she felt her heart beating faster and faster, a still strong voice said, and "Your soul has been anchored."

Hen was sexual harassed and discriminated on her job as a manager. She was wrongfully terminated from her job. Hen was falsely accused on the job. She was so hurt from the ordeal. She became depressed and cried many days and nights. However, one morning a strong voice spoke to her and said, "Weeping may endure just for a night, but joy will come in the morning."

Hen's love for Rooster was unconditional. While working toward her Master's degree, Rooster was working on his plans to be with his recruit. Hen failed one of her courses and was not sure if she would complete her MBA degree. Her carnal heart was broken when she learned from the attorney that Rooster was divorcing her. Hen's mind took her back to all the years of forgiving Rooster. She remembered how she put her relationship with God on the back burner because she listened to the snake and wanted to get even with Rooster. She placed her career goals back stage while caring for her Cockerels and Rooster. Hen's tears became a relief for all the pain, sorrow, and grief; she had experience for more than twenty years.

Hen wanted to take back all of the time she wasted with Rooster, however it was too late. Hen believed that she could *gather, sow, grind, and make a new bread of life* for herself and the cockerels. Through all the turmoil Hen faced, she completes goals one, two, four, five, seven, half of eight, nine, and ten.

Hen, a single mother is determined to complete each of her career goals with the understanding that goal three is beyond her reach. Rooster had to make goal three become real. It takes two people to have a happy marriage.

Hen reached the remainder of her goals, only to be knocked back down again. Hen's new beginning was to provide a new start for those wanting to partake of the new bread. The snake did not want Hen to be successful at allowing others to taste of this new bread. Therefore, the snake with the permission from God attacked Hen as in the *Book of Job* where Satan attacks Job. Hen knew the trap the snake would set for her. She used wisdom to prepare herself for the hurricane she faced.

Hen became ill, depressed, broken, and disgusted. The snake thought Hen had lost her purpose and passion. But he was wrong. Hen explains how faith, forgiveness, love, hope, peace, and tranquility all magnetic forces to her anchor helped her overcome her hurricanes.

The handwriting on Hen's heart started in the dream from her youth. God's grace made Hen a complete woman. Hen's bread was baked and ready to be shared and eaten by those wanting to overcome the hurricanes in his or her personal, professional, or spiritual life.

> *Nay, in all these things we are more than conquerors through him that loved us (Romans 9:37).*

> *I can do all things through Christ who strengthens me (Philippians 4:13).*

Forgiveness

Hen was broken inside from all the hurricanes of her past. For two consecutive years Hen was out of the workforce. This did not stop her purpose and passion. Hen's new business strategy allowed her to give back to her community using her professional skills and abilities. She believed her year of Jubilee was manifested. (Leviticus 25:11). Hen's debt was forgiven.

Hen had difficulty understanding why she hurt so bad and felt so sad when she had forgiven Rooster. She could not understand why the people on her job wanted to see her lose all that she had worked so hard to achieve. Hen knew she was up for a challenge, because the Snake wanted her to die. She used her most powerful weapons to stay alive. (*The Blood of the Lamb, Jesus Christ, the Holy Scriptures, Prayer, Fasting, and Personal Testimonies*) Hen realized this was her opportunity to turn a setback into a comeback.

Hen forgave everyone who hurt her.

> *Father forgive them; for they know not what they do (Luke 23:34).*

> *For the oppression of the poor, for the sighing of the needy, now will I raise, saith the Lord; I will set him in safety from him that puffeth at him (Psalms 12:5).*

Love

Hen's love for mankind is anchored in her heart. This love is not conditional. It does not have a color, sex, nationality, origin, creed, or age. This is not the love experienced on February 14th of each year, but it is shared, 24/7 each day of the year.

People do not understand the love Hen has. Many think she is ill and dying because of the love she has for others. Others think she is lonely, desperate, and has low self-esteem because of this love. The Snake is a Liar. Hen's love is spiritual, therefore to understand it you must operate in the spirit.

Hen practices this love daily in her personal, professional, and spiritual life. Often times she is rejected because others do not understand this love. This love is kind, instructional, informative, giving, sharing, and joyful. Whenever you experience this type of love, you will know it is different from the status quo, I love you if you love me, or love does not love anyone.

One of the ingredients to this love is forgiveness. You cannot love if you have un-forgiveness in your heart. When you love, your thoughts are pure. There is no time to think about negative things because your thought process is focused on positive outcomes. Love covers a multitude of hurt, pain, and sin. Everyone can love. It does not cost anything to open up your heart and love one another.

Faith

Faith is based on truth, which will come to past. Your tongue guards your faith. In other words, whenever you set goals for yourself, speak to the goal and include the time of completion. Spiritually, faith is a belief in God's Word that he promises and that it is truth.

In the story, Hen had faith. She put God first in her life. Everything else she did was centered on her faith. Hen's faith helped her achieve her goals. Faith is manifested in the power of positive thinking. Doubt to faith is like water to a fire, it kills. Never allow doubt to kill your faith. Faith is obedience to God's Word.

As the woman with the issue of blood for twelve years believed if she touched the hem of Jesus garment she would be whole, her faith made her whole.

> *Daughter, be of good comfort; thy faith hath made thee whole (Matthew 9:22)*

Peace

Peace is supernatural. It cannot be moved by the natural or carnal mind. Whenever, Hen had perfect peace she was spiritually minded. Peace guards the mind from snake attacks. Peace places the flesh under submission to the Will and Word of God.

Peace is the opposite of controversy or strife. Peace is a quiet humble spirit. Peace is freedom and cannot be oppressed. Peace is clean, holy, and pure. Peace walks in love. It is gentle and calm. Peace is oneness in spirit and never divided.

> *The Lord lifts up his countenance upon thee, and gives thee peace (Numbers 6:27).*

Hope

Hope is seeing the light at the end of the tunnel. Many relate hope to having a vision toward accomplishing a goal or business strategy. Hope is the believing in an outcome that is not within reach. Hope is the will to believe. It is also what the Word of God promises as an outcome or a good benefit. Hope is the will power within oneself to make sacrifices toward achieving goals.

Never give up on hope. Hope allows you to get up each day to function as a good citizen. Because of hope, you believe that working toward your goals will allow you to reap a good harvest. Hope is an expectation. When you have faith, you are keeping hope alive within your heart, mind, and soul.

> *But I will hope continually, and will yet praise thee more and more (Psalms 71: 14).*

> *And hope maketh not ashamed; because the love of God is shed abroad in our hearts by the Holy Ghost which is given unto us (Romans 5:5).*

Tranquility

Tranquility is a form of contentment. Tranquility is manifested by having calm and peaceful behavior. At the end of Hen's process to turn the grain of wheat into a loaf of bread she found tranquility. She was able to invite her family and friends to partake of the new bread. Hen was under attack by the snake multiple times before she reached tranquility. The hurricanes did not stop raging in Hen's life until she found tranquility.

Under the influence of the snake, Hen sought after love in the wrong places. She was at her lowest point when the hurricanes came in to destroy her. Hen explained, "All my life, whenever I would find peace, the snake would come and steal it." Yet, whenever she realized the power of her tongue and the strength she had in the Living Word of God her tranquility could not be removed. Hen explained, "I am as a baby in the bosom of her mother, whenever I experience tranquility; it is though I have no cares of this world."

> *Ye are of God, little children, and have overcome them: because greater is he that is in you, than he that is in the world (1 John 4:4.)*

> *Be not overcome of evil, but overcome evil with good (Romans 12:21).*

Discussion

You must keep your anchor in position at all times because you do not want a hurricane to take you by surprise. The Hen had an anchor, however in the story; she allowed her anchor to be moved. The Hen allowed the snake to speak to the carnal man. Once the thoughts were implanted into the carnal man's thinking process, the Hen reacted upon those thoughts.

Pessimist's behavior is depicted as the carnal man. He does not allow his spiritual man to operate in his life.

Rooster never allowed the spirit man to operate in his life. Optimist honored both his mother and father. He did good deeds in his community, but did he fully operate in the spirit?

_____

_____

_____

_____

Which characters in the story describes you?

What can you do now to change the outcomes of your hurricanes and improve your life?

_____

_____

_____

_____

_____

_____

Five Simple Steps to Releasing Your Anchor: Personal and Professional Development

Using the five simple steps to release your anchor can promote personal and professional growth. These steps can allow you to understand who you are and what you want to become. Successful application of the five steps can help you grow into the leader you want to become.

(1). Complete an internal assessment of yourself.

(2). Identify what you want to change in your life.

(3). Write down the steps you must take to make this change happen.

(4). Monitor your progress and ensure you are content with the change in your life.

(5). Make a positive difference in the lives of others.

Spiritual Development

Today is your day. This is your moment to stop letting the snake prevent you from reaching each and every goal you have set in your life. Now is the time to design your *anchor*. Recall, your *anchor* is your spiritual man. The spiritual man is your soul. To design your spiritual man, you must understand your carnal man.

The spirit man is lead by the Holy Ghost yet, the carnal man has not grown into the fullness of God's Holy Spirit. The carnal man is still a babe in Christ. To design your anchor, take the steps as follows:

Steps to Design Your Anchor

1. Love the Father and His Son with all your heart mind and soul (Matthew 22:37)

2. Love thy neighbor as thyself (Matthew 22:39)

3. Let the Holy Spirit lead and guide your life

4. Get rid of selfishness

5. Get rid of pride

6. Walk in faith, love, hope, peace, and tranquility

7. Read the Word of God for Understanding

Steps to Design Your Anchor Continued

8. Keep the Word of God Hidden, Rooted, and Grounded in Your Heart

9. Pray daily (Matthew 6:9-13) Other scriptures based on the obstacles you may be facing (The Book of Psalms)

10. Do not let anyone steal what God has promised you

11. Let your tongue speak only life and those things that are good and positive

12. Use wisdom in your decision making process

13. Write out your goals and create a realistic time frame for completion

14. Reset goals that are not met and achieve your goals

Defining Your Success

Success is in the eye of the beholder. Never let someone else define your success. Hen did not let her accomplishments define her success. Nor did she let her hurricanes prevent her success. Her success was driven by her purpose and passion to inspire the lives of others. Allowing success to become self-centered based on research has proven to be the reason so many leaders have derailed.

Leadership is not selfish, it should be about followership. When reaching to climb the ladder of success, set a vision for the well-being of others. No major organization became successful by creating a product or service for him or her solely. If the success of an organization was based on the visionary, without a purpose, the vision would not be fulfilled.

You can succeed without having to make others look smaller than yourself. Whenever, you reach the top bring someone else up with you. Hen's measurement and implementation of Success:

Strategize= Goals; when creating your goals develop a strategy for goal completion.

Understanding= Life- long learning; continue life-long learning from a variety of inspirational and positive sources which are linked to your spiritual, personal, and professional growth.

Creating= Motivation and Persistence; motivation leads to persistence and both are required to create a new idea or vision designed for a great purpose.

Communicating=Networking; your network must include those who understand and support your vision and mission. Communicating your mission to supporters will enhance their lives toward a positive unselfish purpose.

Evaluating=Integrity; paves your future as a great leader. Constant evaluation and repentance births a person of new beginnings.

Strengthen=Self-Discipline; is your strength. You will grow and become strengthen by living the true Words of God.

Surpass= Community and Professionalism; community outreach is accomplished through dedication and professionalism. Surpassing all hurricanes provide you the ability to inspire others through love.

Dialog

Embrace each day as a journey in which you have full control. Life never stops, neither should you? Never let any situation or circumstance defeat your thought process to produce negative outcomes. You are a positive force whom can impact the lives of other people.

Whenever you are faced with adversity, stare it in the face and speak the words of your positive outcome. Do not let your current negative state prevent you from reaching your future positive accomplishments.

Hold on to your dreams and never stop dreaming. If you do not have any dreams, create some positive dreams which include you reaching forward into your community to inspire others.

You must grow personally, professionally, and spiritually. You were not created to be a baby for your entire life. Whenever a baby comes home with his or her parents, they are fully responsible for the caring for the baby because the baby can do nothing for him or herself.

Notwithstanding, the baby goes through the stages of development and begins to crawl, walk, talk, eat, develop a personality, etc. The development goes from baby, newborn, infant, and toddler. Each of these stages is reflective of the beginning of an individual's development.

Development Theory

The theory of Erik Erikson (1902-1994) discussed stages of development as we may have experienced ourselves or in the lives of others. These stages noted as, follows:

(1) Infancy- Birth to 18 months: Ego Development Outcome: Trust and Mistrust; Basic Strengths: Drive and Hope

(2) Early Childhood- 18 month to 3 years; Ego Development Outcome: Autonomy versus Shame; Basic Strengths: Self-control, Courage and Will

(3) Play Age- 3 to 5 years: Ego Development Outcome: Initiative versus Guilt; Basic Strength: Purpose

(4) School Age-16-12 years; Ego Development Outcome: Industry versus Inferiority. Basic Strengths: Method and Competence

(5) Adolescence- 12 to 18 years; Ego Development Outcome: Identity versus Role Confusion; Basic Strengths: Devotion and Fidelity

(6) Young Adulthood- 18 to 35 years; Ego Development Outcome: Intimacy and Solidarity versus Isolation

(7) Middle Adulthood-35 to 55 or 65; Ego Development Outcome: Generatively versus Self-Absorption or Stagnation; Basic Strengths: Production and Care

(8) Late Adulthood-55 or 65 to Death; Integrity versus Despair; Basic Strength: Wisdom

The theory of Erikson supports the theory of Dr. Paulette Howard Burney's in the short story of each character.

Theory Application

At one point in the story Pessimist age of 12 was revealed, however none of the other characters ages were revealed. Dr Burney asked a question on page 75.

Which character in the story describes you? Dr. Burney's response to the question: I am the Hen. This story is based on real experiences of Dr, Paulette Howard Burney. She experienced each of Erickson's stages of development. She observed the stages of development of Rooster and the cockerels. The Hen's stages of development were completed earlier than the chronological order of Erickson's theory. Although she is not in late adulthood, Dr, Burney is a woman of wisdom and integrity as examined in the story as the Hen.

In the story, the cockerel's development is a reflection of the relationship of the family's nurturing, spiritual, and social environments. However, Dr.

Burney's assumption is the cockerels did not master their basic strengths in early childhood. An assumption is also made that the Rooster did not master certain stages or chose to become self-absorbed. He forgot about his immediate family as a loving and devoting husband to his wife or caring and nurturing father to his sons.

Recall in the story is about a military family. Military families face a lot of *change* based on the constant relocating. The military family is most often separated from family, friends, and loves ones. They most often must make new friends and adapt to different environments quickly. Optimist was able to adapt and meet new friends easily. He was conceived when Hen and Rooster were first married. The Hen was happy during this time and Rooster was a devoted and faithful husband. However, when Pessimist was conceived Hen and Rooster were having marriage problems.

Because of the constant change an issue with Pessimist adapting. After the divorce, the Hen told Pessimist about her struggles while he was in her womb.

Unborn in the Womb

Dr. Burney, explained, "Pessimist was 12 years old and he was impacted most negatively by the divorce." Her assumption is Pessimist did not have trust from birth because while he was in Hen's womb, she did not experience trust with Rooster. At one point in the story Hen wanted to commit suicide because she lost drive and hope to live. She was depressed and stressed.

Several years earlier, prior to Pessimist leaving for the military, Hen told him the story of her depression and explained how special and dear to her heart he was to her. She told him how much she loved him so much and wanted to watch him grow into being a positive and great citizen.

Whenever the Hen was with child with Pessimist she saw a black crow hanging from the roof of their home in England. The prophets in the church told Hen, the crow was symbolic of wanting the soul of her unborn child.

The Hen gave birth and proclaims the birth of her son a gift from God. He is a child born with a purpose. Pessimist name is changed to *Victory*.

Notwithstanding, The Hen learns from her mother that while she was in her mother's womb, her mother experienced issue with Hen's father which caused her to feel depressed and stressed. Hen's father had extra-marital affairs, stayed out all night with his women, and did not provide for Hen's mother or the other siblings. This is the reason the Hen came home from the hospital with her mother only and her mother and father never lived together as a family with their children.

Rooster was reared in a single parent home. He often expressed his anger against his father because he was not in the household helping his mother care for them. Rooster's father had extra-marital affairs.

Dr. Burney's assumption is supported by researchers that individuals will have difficulty developing and having the basic strengths of growth whenever the mother does not experience love, hope, joy, trust, and happiness while the child is carried in the womb.

Supporting Research to Hen's Assumption

Dr. Elizabeth Carman, PhD, and Neil J. Carman, PhD, Cosmic Cradle topic of *Unwanted in the Womb* notes the research of Goteborg, Sweden, Dr. David B. Chamberlain, and Dr. Andrew Feldmar whom all affirm the assumptions made in the story. Because Hen experienced so much depression, stress, mistrust, etc. from Rooster their unborn child was birth with anger, hurt, lack of self-control, lack of purpose, affiliation, and love. However, by the Grace of God and the Blood of the Lamb he is set free.

> *John the Baptist was filled with the Holy Ghost even from his mother's womb*
> *(Luke 2:16; Luke 1:41).*

Now it is Time to Release Your Anchor

Exercise-One

Write a list of situations or circumstances preventing you from reaching you personal, professional, or spiritual goals. Use additional paper as needed to complete your list.

1. _____
2. _____
3. _____
4. _____
5. _____

Second create a list of what you want to change in your personal, professional, and spiritual life. Use additional paper as needed to complete this list.

1. _____
2. _____
3. _____
4. _____
5. _____

Third make a list of three short term goals you want to reach within 3 to six months; and two long term goals you want to complete within 12 to 36 months.

3-6 Month Goals

1. _____
2. _____
3. _____

12-36 Month Goals

1. _____
2. _____
3. _____

After completion of the self-evaluation process, create a career plan for yourself.

(A). Apply the *SUCCESS* model defined on pages 69-70 and the Steps for Development on Page 76.

(B). Describe the plan you will create to achieve your short term and long term goals using the model outlined.

(C). Develop and include in your career plan an instrument to measure the effectiveness of your goals and whether these goals are attainable and realistic.

(D). Include alternatives, time-frames, and the procedures you will use to reach both short-term and long-term goals.

(E). Share your personal career plan with someone you trust. Identify someone who will support and coach you toward reaching your goals. Share your professional career goals with a mentor and your supervisor. Share your spiritual goals with a person who shares the same faith and beliefs as yourself.

Exercise- Two

(A). Create your mission statement.

(B). Create your vision statement.

(C). Your vision and mission statements should align with both your short term and long term goals.

(D). Share these statements with individuals whom will support your mission and vision.

Mission Statement

Vision Statement

Exercise- Three

Create your definition of *SUCCESS*. The creation of your success should include the knowledge learned and experienced from the previous exercises.

The outcome from exercises one through three is a result of you releasing your anchor. You already have the positive attributes inside of you. However, they cannot be birthed until your anchor is released.

I challenge you to *Release Your Anchor*.

Define Success

Place This in Your Heart

Certificate of Excellence

is hereby presented by

God the Father through Jesus Christ

To

Speak Your Name

For my sins and the sins of the world, through faith; believing that Jesus Christ died and rose on the third day. I am asking for forgiveness of my sins and I have been baptized in water for the remission of my sins.

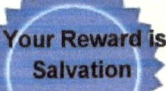

Witnessed by: Father, Son, and Holy Ghost

The Promise

The promise is we may have whatsoever we ask because of our Lord and Saviour Jesus Christ whom died for our sins gave us the promise. Operating in this promise is how Hen continues to face the tribulations of her journey.

> *Jesus said, (For after all these things do the Gentiles seek :) for your heavenly Father knoweth that ye have need of all these things (Matthew 6:32).*

God's Promise to Us through Abraham

> *The Lord said to Abraham...And in thy seed shall all of the nations of the earth be blessed because thou hast obeyed my voice (Genesis 22:18).*

The bow shall be in the cloud; and I will look upon it, that I may remember the everlasting covenant between God and every living creature of all flesh that is upon the earth (Genesis 9:16).

Conclusion

Hurricanes will come and they will go. Ensure your anchor is grounded and secure. You will know when it is time to *Release Your Anchor* to conquer all your hurricanes. You must remember to keep your anchor in position at all times. Because hurricanes come swiftly and often times there is minimal time to prepare for your hurricane.

Love, faith, hope, peace, and tranquility are key inspirational magnetic forces to ensure the purposeful release of your anchor. You can accomplish all goals in your spiritual, personal, and professional life because you have an anchor and understand how to release it.

References

Harder, A.F. MA, MFT (2012). *The developmental stages of erik erickson*, The information in this article comes from *Childhood and Society* by Erik Erickson as well as from noted took in Phillips Graduate Institute, previously California Family Study Center. Retrieved from http://www.support4change.com

Carman, E. PhD, Carman N.J. PhD. (2003). Unwanted *in the womb*. Retrieved from http://www.cosmiccradle.com. Souls waiting in the wings for birth.

All scripture quotations unless otherwise noted are taken from the *Holy Bible* King James Version.

About the Author

My passion for assisting others toward reaching spiritual, personal and professional goals birthed my vision as the founder and President of P&B Developing Leaders. As a scholar practitioner, I have worked in the Business Administration for more than twenty years and have served internationally in the business field in Iraq, Greece, and England; Former College Chair for School of Business for University of Phoenix. Currently serve as a committee member for the School of Advanced Studies for University of Phoenix.

Dr. Burney is a creative, adventurous, passionate professor, currently teaching for Saint Leo University; former Senate Committee- member. Twenty years of professional experience in business administration include the fields of management, consulting, education, personnel development, curriculum design, training, human resources, managerial finance, and accounting.

The past twelve years my contributions to the field of education include teaching at Axia of University of Phoenix, University of Phoenix Atlanta Campus, Western International University, Strayer University, Saint Leo University, Central Texas College, and the Ministerial Training and Development Center in Iraq. Courses taught in the MBA program include Strategic Management, International Business, and Leadership. Undergraduates courses taught include but are not limited to Financial and Managerial Accounting, Psychology, Business, Economics, Management, Research Writing, Computer Information Systems, Human Resources Management, Government Accounting, Budget Programming and Management. I served a Business Public School Educator in Texas and Georgia. I earned my Doctoral degree in business with a major in Organizational Management/ leadership, from Capella University, with a Professional Human Resource Management Certification from University of Phoenix. MBA, at Tarleton University, and B.S. in Business Administration at Troy University.

Visit my website at pbdevelopingleaders.com.

Words of Encouragement

All is well within my soul. The words in this story were presented to inspire anyone who may be going through a hurricane in his or her life. The words are based on real-life experiences of a military family whom faced many hurricanes and continues to strive for internal peace within their souls to surpass all natural understanding. Dr. Paulette Howard Burney releases her unconditional compassion to everyone who reads this story that your hearts will be blessed and you too will be filled with compassion toward others.

Genesis 1:26; (Understand that God created everything for his purpose and he created you in his image and his likeness)

And God said; Let us make man in our image, after our likeness:

Proverbs 16:4

The Lord hath made all things for himself: yea, even the wicked for the day of evil.

Romans 11:36 (Understand Your Reason for Existence)

For him, and through him, and to him, are all things; to whom be glory forever. Amen

John 14:16 (When you feel lonely and want to give up know that God the Father sent his Son Jesus and he left you with a Comforter. You are never alone.)

Jesus said, and I will pray the Father, and he shall give you another Comforter, that he may abide with you forever.

Psalm 35:1-4

(1)Plead my cause, O Lord, with them that strive with me: fight against them that fight against me. (2)Take hold of shield and buckler, and stand up for mine help. (3)Draw out also the spear, and stop the way against them that persecute me: say unto my soul, I am thy salvation.

Psalm 34:1-4

(1)I will bless the Lord at all times; his praise shall continually be in my mouth. (2)My soul shall make her boast in the Lord: the humble shall hear thereof, and be glad. (3) O magnify the Lord with me, and let us exalt his name together. (4)I sought the Lord, and he heard me, and delivered me from all my fears.

Matthew 5: 44 (Let *love conquer every situation you face in life*)

Jesus said, but I say unto you, Love your enemies, bless them that curse you, do good to them that hate you, and pray for them which despitefully use you, and persecute you

Matthew 26: 41 *(Pray daily to remain humble to live out your Godly purpose).*

Watch and pray that ye enter not into temptation: the spirit indeed is willing, but the flesh is weak.

Psalms 37:39-40 (If you sin or become troubled, repent and get back up because your God loves you and he will never let you down)

(39) But the salvation of the righteous is of the Lord: he is their strength in time of trouble. (40) And the Lord shall help them, and deliver them from the wicked, and save them, because they trust in him.

Psalms 71:1-2 (Know that you can trust God to bring you through every situation in your life)

(1)In thee, O Lord, do I put my trust: let me never be put to confusion. (2)Deliver me in thy righteousness, and cause me to escape: incline thine ear unto me, and save me.

Psalms 102:1-2

(1)Hear my prayer, O Lord, and let my cry come unto thee. (2)Hide not thy face from me in the day when I am in trouble; incline thine ear unto me: in the day when I can answer me speedily.

Matthew 5:3-11(Develop a character of unmovable love; in which you become a leader with integrity)

Blessed are the poor in spirit: for theirs is the kingdom of heaven (Humility)

Blessed are they that mourn: for they shall be comforted (Satisfaction)

Blessed are they which do hunger and thirst after righteousness: for they shall be filled (Salvation)

Blessed are the pure in heart: for they shall see God (Sincerity)

Blessed are the peacemakers: for they shall be called the children of God (Love)

Blessed are they which are persecuted for righteousness sake: for theirs is the kingdom of heaven (Obedience)

Blessed are ye, when men shall revile you, and persecute you, and shall say all manner of evil against you falsely, for my sake (Faith)

II Timothy 2:22 (When you become tempted as Jesus did by Satan, call on the Name of Jesus, the Blood of the Lamb; will strengthen you to do the right thing.

Flee also youthful lusts: but follow righteousness, faith, charity, peace, with them that call on the Lord out of a pure heart.

I Corinthians 10:13

There hath no temptation taken you but such as is common to man: but God is faithful, who above that ye are able; but will with the temptation also make a way to escape, that ye may be able to bear it.

Revelation 2:5 (No matter how badly you mess up, always repent so that your sins may be forgiven)

Jesus said, *Remember therefore from whence thou art fallen, and repent, and do the first works; or else I will come unto thee quickly. And will remove thy candlestick out of this place, except thou repent.*

Words of Wisdom from the Author

Whenever an evil thought comes to your mind, refocus that thought to a positive outcome. Think on positive and good things at all times. All things that happen start from the mind. As humans we naturally move toward what we focus our attention to. The more you think about something, the greater the opportunity for it to overtake you.

Temptation starts by getting your attention. Once your attention is caught your emotions will arise. Then it is your emotions which will cause you to act out a certain behavior, you will act on what you felt. Often times, the more you focus on not wanting to do something, the temptation becomes stronger.

When something tempts you ignore it. Once your mind is on something else, the temptation loses its power. When temptation calls you on the telephone, hang it up. When temptation knocks on your door or rings your door bell, do not answer it. When temptation flirts with you for the cause of fornication or adultery, run away from it. When temptation places you in a situation to defame your character or integrity, do whatever is necessary to turn your attention to something else.

Spiritually, your mind is the most defenseless organs. Apply the Word of God to replace all evil thoughts. You will overcome evil with good.

www.ingramcontent.com/pod-product-compliance
Lightning Source LLC
Chambersburg PA
CBHW042218240426
43670CB00034B/13